# BECOMING A MONEY MAGNET

**GBEMINIYI EBODA**

# BECOMING
# A MONEY
# MAGNET

**BECOMING A MONEY MAGNET**

Copyright 2006 by Gbeminiyi Eboda
ISBN 978-978-951-387-1


**MOVE YOUR WORLD INT'L.**
P.O. Box 21089, U.I. Ibadan, Oyo State

First Print 2006
Second Print 2009
Third Print 2015

For further enquiries, visit:
www.moveurworld.com

Designed by
GreenKnight Solutions
+234 802 346 9942

**AQUA**PUB

# ACKNOWLEDGMENT

Tunde Wale-Temowo, you are a son of sorts, a value adder and a plus factor. Please know that the God who sees in the secret will certainly reward in the open.

Tayo Ogunleye, you polished the rough diamond, packaged it and gave it an audience acceptability and market value. I see your dream fructify.

Pastors in HCC, my wife and I treasure your alliance with the vision which is nothing but a personal obedience to the call. I deeply appreciate the fact that we know where we are going, you know that we are well on the way and you know that we have been made for arrival.

The esteemed members of HCC at home and in diaspora, it is a rare honour to be a coach to a rare kind of people, models destined to be leaders labels in their generation!

# CONTENT

CHAPTER ONE

# BE A
# VALUE-ADDER

EVERYDAY 1.3 TRILLION DOLLARS MOVE around the world in an electronic form. Everyday, tens of billions of naira circulate around our country as people exchange money for the purchase of essentials like transportation, food, toiletries, etc.

By the close of the day, all these monies end up in different accounts and houses where they are domiciled. They may travel through many hands but they end up somewhere with someone. What is the drawing power? What makes cash travel from an address in search of another? The answer is very simple – IT IS VALUE.

People pay for value and not for cheap. When a man is employed, his remuneration is usually a reflection of his perceived value in the eyes of his employer. When people pay for a product or service, the amount they are willing to pay is directly a function of the value attached to such a product or service. People are generally paid in life in direct proportion to the work they do, how well they do it, and how difficult it is to get a replacement for them.

Therefore, to be rich, become a value-adder. Add value to yourself and to your work. Remember that your work is an extension of who you are. It is the lengthened shadow of your capability. Give more than you are being paid for. Work longer than the agreed schedule. Deliver more than is expected – it makes you indispensable. It makes you irreplaceable and it makes you unforgettable. When an up line vacancy shows up, you will be the first to be recommended for promotion. In the event of downsizing, you will be the last to be considered for retrenchment.

The extra mile is a road less traveled and hardly patronized. It therefore becomes easy to be noticed when your performance becomes exceptional. Your ovation in life will be directly proportional to your donations. Become an active participant in your life's upward mobility. Move your contributions with diligence to that place where the resources and increase of the land can gracefully walk into your hands.

CHAPTER TWO

# THE POWER TO PRODUCE

THE VERY FIRST INSTRUCTION THAT GOD gave to man in the scriptures is a seven letter word, *'produce'*. It was neither a suggestion nor an advice. It was an instruction. You can call it the premier command; **BE FRUITFUL.** You can only call out of a thing what is within it, which implies that the power to produce is inherent in our make-up and embedded in our design.

Barrenness is an aberration and not a normalcy. To be fruitless is a curse. If you are familiar with scriptures, you will remember the story of the fig tree. The power to bring forth was withdrawn from it by a curse. If the power to bring forth can be terminated by a curse, it means that the same power will need to be initiated by a blessing.

We are told in the first chapter of the first book of the bible, and in the twenty-eighth verse that God blessed the first couple. He blessed them and said to them 'be fruitful', which means you cannot be fruitful without the blessing.

Isn't that good news for us? If you know the Lord, you will realize it is good news for us for it is written in His word, "Blessed be God and Father of our Lord Jesus Christ, who has blessed us with all spiritual blessings in heavenly places", so, you are already blessed!

If you are blessed, it means that you have the power to produce. You have all it takes to bring forth. God has no tolerance for unfruitfulness. Life itself only endures the fruitless and will hiss and never miss the exit of the man or woman who is not productive. To be productive is to make your existence consequential and beneficial. To be productive is to make your contributions significant and noticeable. To be productive is to justify your duration with your donations and to complement longevity with productivity.

You must realize that money is always a consequence and never a coincidence. Those who have it, make it. So, to *want it* or even *need it*, is not enough. You must be willing to *make it*. Others have made it and you can make it too. Remember that money is a reward for what you produce. How then do you produce?

1.  Recognize that you have been empowered by the

blessing of God to prosper.

2. Know that you are loaded; for only the 'seed-full can be fruitful'. So, discover your seeds.

3. Develop your gift. A gift without skill equals performance without reward. Add value to your gift; it is called 'skill'. Skill repositions a gift from a local platform to a global stage.

Finally, be your best – work hard and work smart. The only substitute for hard work may be a hard life. Put premium effort into your vocation. The harder you work, the luckier you get. Justify the privilege of your existence every time you wake up and every time your feet touch the ground. Get moving; get going; get running. It may not come to where you are, but it can't stop you from reaching where it is. Go for it. It is your time.

CHAPTER THREE

# THE PRINCIPLE OF THE SEED

I N THE EIGHTH CHAPTER OF THE FIRST BOOK of the bible and in the twenty-second verse, it is written that as long as the earth remains, seed time and harvest shall not cease.

It is assumed in the context of this scripture that the reader knows that for there to be a seed, then there should be a sower. This brings to mind a very important truth; the value of the seed lies in its ability to be sown.

The value of a seed begins at the point when it is sown. "For except a grain of wheat falls to the ground and dies, it abides alone." A seed is a prediction of a man's tomorrow. God gives bread to the eater and seed to the sower. It is wisdom on your part to recognize the difference between your seed and your bread. Your seed is your right to the future. Your seed usually and ultimately attracts the favour of God. There should never be a time in a man's life when he is without a seed.

Every seed has a future, it is called the harvest and the future has a mandate to play host, not only to the harvest, but also to the reaper. The future, under the influence of time processes the seed into a harvest and transforms the sower into the reaper. The favour on the seed thus becomes the favour on the reaper. We therefore never pity a man with a seed. It is a man without a seed, the one who has eaten his seed that should be pitied.

We don't pity the sower; we simply encourage him or her to hold on and not to give up. We pray for him or her to hold on and not to give up on the eve of their coronation; not to plant for others to reap. We remind them of God's exceedingly great and precious promise that he who goes forth weeping and bearing precious seeds shall without doubt return with rejoicing bringing his sheaves with him.

For any sower to enter into their harvest, they will need to cross the bridge of TIME. However, not everybody makes it across this bridge. "For you have need of patience so that after you have done the will of God, you will eventually inherit His promises." One of the symptoms that inform a man that he is close to his season of harvest is fatigue and a sense of weariness.

When a man wants to give up, then he is close to his dream's dawn. Are you feeling down? Are you feeling like throwing in the towel? Are you feeling like giving up? It simply means you are close to your desired harvest and God's word to you today is to hold on. For yet a little while, you are going to step into your season of rejoicing and laughter as you enter into your promised harvest.

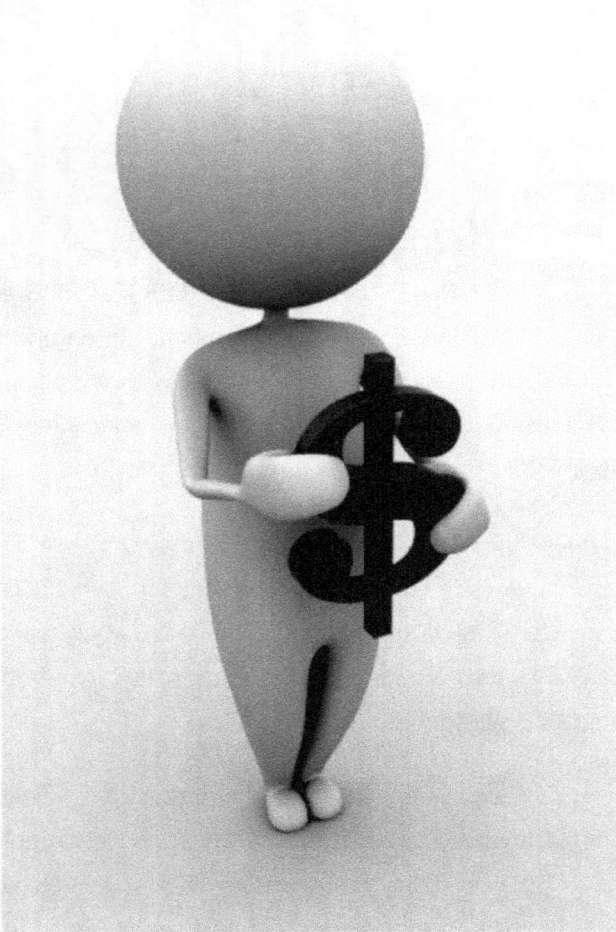

CHAPTER FOUR

# MONEY MATTERS

**M**ONEY INDEED REALLY MATTERS. IT HAS been rightly observed that a man is not free until he is economically free. Money gives you options; it gives you freedom. Money allows you to make significant contributions.

It was Rockefeller, one time world's richest man that said "I must make money, and after making money, I must make much more, and then I must make much, much more. My conscience cannot allow me not to make money, for there is no way you can help humanity without money".

With your money, you can stop the mourning of several orphans, widows and the less privileged. A lot of people have various misconceptions about money. For example, some people believe that money is evil. Some even go ahead to say that money is the root of all evil. That is simply not true. Money has no morality of its own. It is neither good nor bad. It simply assumes the morality of its current custodian.

Some also believe that money changes people. This is also quite untrue. Money never determines who you are; it only reveals who you are. When a fool becomes rich, he becomes a rich fool. Others also believe that there is no money. This is a false insinuation. There is no scarcity of money. All the money from Adam through Solomon the wise king of Israel down to our contemporary world has only been increasing. The problem is not the existence of money but its residence.

Once upon a time in the days when there were no water purifiers, a ship went on a voyage and customarily took drinkable water along in barrels. The crew took enough water by their estimation, to last for the duration of the voyage. However, the journey became longer than anticipated until all the drinkable water was exhausted. The captain of the ship climbed the deck and seeing an expanse of sea water all around him, cried out in exasperation, "water, water everywhere, but none to drink."

The same applies to the issue of money. There is money everywhere. How to make the money yours should be your concern. There are wealth conductors; we have low conductors and high conductors. Subsequently, we will be discussing how to be a money magnet. With money, you can indeed make significant contributions.

CHAPTER FIVE

# FINANCIAL INTELLIGENCE

TO BE RICH, I NEED TO HAVE FINANCIAL intelligence. By this, I mean I must be able to separate and define an asset from a liability. A liability is anything that takes money from my pocket, while an asset is anything that puts money in my pocket.

To be rich, I do not need more money; what I need is more wisdom. That is why when you meet the rich, do not ask for what is in their hands, rather seek to know what is on their minds.

It has been empirically proven that most jackpot winners return to their original financial status within nine months to one year of winning the jackpot. Why? The reason is very simple when your money goes up and your mind or wisdom doesn't go up, your money will shrink back to the size of your wisdom.

A major key to becoming wealthy therefore, is to become a protégé of and not a parasite on the rich. This is very simple, the protégé wants what you have learnt, but the parasite wants what you have earned. Yet, your learning is responsible for your earnings. To earn, I must learn, and to learn, I must yearn. So, my earning prowess is a function of my learning posture, which is also a function of my yearning tendency.

I must increase my passion to know. I must increase my hunger to know more. Never forget that to quest for, is to become the best of. So, become a student of the rich, for there is no way a man will walk with giants, eat what they eat and remain a dwarf. Read what they read, listen to the things they listen to and let your choices be informed by your new exposure. There is a predictable outcome; your days of lack will soon become history.

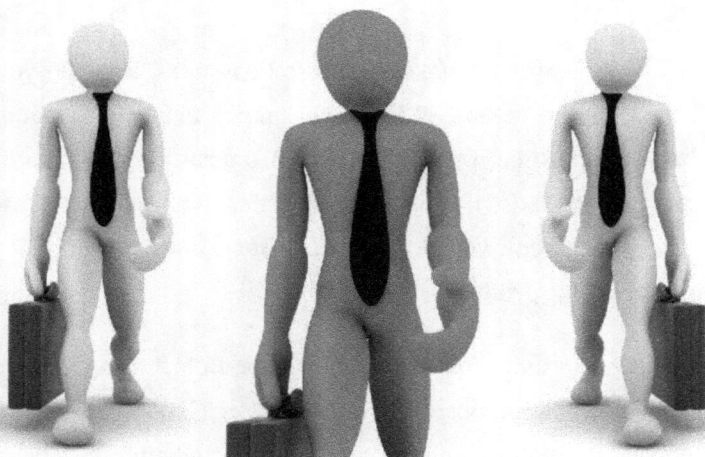

CHAPTER SIX

# GET
# BUSY

God hates idleness. He loves busy-ness. How do you define business? It simply means being busy doing something profitable. Not just busy for the sake of being busy, because if you are chit chatting, whiling away time, or roaming about, you are certainly busy, but obviously not doing anything profitable.

God supports that the idle should starve. In fact, He supports that the idle should not survive for He says in His word that he that does not work should not eat. If God is against the idle, it explains why everything is against the idle. Things only get worse for the idle. Until a man takes the initiative, his value will be depreciating. To live without doing is to be dying without knowing.

A man who does not work will be a burden; though he was created to be a blessing. My question to you and multitudes of my country men who are believing God for something but not doing anything with their lives is 'why die a liability, when God has created you to be an asset?' "Why stand ye idle all day?" was the question of the vineyard owner in Matthew 20 to a group of men that were found idle in the market place. The lesson is very simple – God frowns at a day's idleness. Yet, many have been idle, not just for a day, a week or a month but for years!

As far as heaven is concerned, there should be no day without hay. *Everyday you make no 'hay' is one in which you are not fit for a pay.* Your productive input on a daily basis is the only way to announce your continued existence.

Why are people jobless? Well, I think I have a few reasons for that:

1. They do not realize it is a crime to be jobless.

2. They are expecting too much from others maybe from friends, uncles, aunts or even the government.

3. They are allowing their certificates to limit their money-making opportunities. They feel some jobs do not fit their certificates or their status. Yet, the certificates that **fit** them have not been able to **feed** them.

4.  They don't know that time is going. Understand that you are not getting younger.

Our destinies are in our hands. If we must find, we shall have to seek. The man in the SUV is not better than the man on the street, he has only taken the steps the other man is afraid of taking.

There are things your heart longs to do, but there are things your hands find to do. The bible says "whatever your hand finds to do, do it with all your might." Don't start out in life being choosy. Just be busy making profit. Later, you can be choosy. Do not be too big to do small things; else you will be too small to do big things.

Start from whatever your hand finds to do on the way to what your mind wants to do. Remember, no place is too insignificant to start from since you will not remain there. Start and don't stop moving; you will get there!

CHAPTER SEVEN

# STEP OUT
# AND STEP UP

STEP OUT OF YOUR FEARS; THE WORLD IS AT your feet. Step out of your limitations. There is more to you than meets the eye. Step out of your past, your best of days are not behind you; they are ahead of you.

Step out of the regrets of your mistakes. Those who are afraid of making mistakes actually never make anything at all. Mistakes are simply a part of our discoveries on the way to success. A mistake is one of the prices we pay when we embrace the spirit of adventure.

Step out of your comfort zone, for the enemy of the *next* is what we have termed the *best*. Step out of your security, for it can keep you in obscurity. In life, there is really nothing like security; there is only freedom. Step out of the limitations of your gender, success is gender blind. Step out of the limitations of your background, success is neither genetic nor is failure hereditary. Your background has no right to keep your back on the ground.

Step out of the limitations of your skin colour, black is not synonymous with lack. Step out of the limitations of your age, age is not an index of respect in the race of life. In life, there are no age mates; there are only illumination colleagues. If you are young, your age should not restrict you, and if you are old, neither should your age retire you.

Step out of your tradition; it is an enemy of innovations. Step out of your failure, it should only improve the future; not imprison it. Step out of your success. Never mistake progress for arrival, and never confuse a bus-stop for the end-stop. Step out of all you have been. Dare for more, as you step out, you will definitely step up. I believe in your success.

CHAPTER EIGHT

# THE MEASURE
# OF TRUE SUCCESS

SUCCESS IS NOT JUST ABOUT REACHING your goals; it's about helping others to reach theirs too. Success is not just about climbing up; it is about lifting others up. Success is not what happens on the outside; it is what happens within. Success isn't just known by the harvest; it is first known by the seeds. Success is not what we pursue; it is what we attract as a result of who we become.

Success is not about where you started; it is about where you finish. It's not about where you began, it's about where you end. Success is not just about where you arrived, it's about how you arrived. Success is not about what you got, it's about how you got it. Success is not about what you have achieved, it's about who you have become.

Success is not about making money; it is about making meaning. It is not getting ahead of others; it is about self leadership. It is not making a living; it is getting a life. It is not reaching a destination; it is enjoying the journey.

It is not simply about achievement; it is largely about contentment. It is not getting what you want; it is wanting what you got. It is not just about what you know; it is also about who you know. It is not about having no needs; it is being in control of your moods, in spite of the needs. It is not success if it is at the expense of others.

Success is not measured by the container; it is usually measured by the content. Face value can be a false value. Today, I dare you to check your value system. For the extent of your success will be determined by the content of your belief system.

Re-appraise your values; experience a paradigm shift. Move in the direction of God's will for your life. Make up your mind to finish, to finish strong and to finish well. May the grace of God make the difference in your race through life. May you arrive at the place of your celebration.

CHAPTER NINE

# THE FORCE
# OF COURAGE

A S WE TRAVEL THROUGH LIFE, MANY things will certainly happen to us, but the greatest determinant of success is not what happens to us, but what happens within us. That's why it's been wisely said that what lies behind us and what lies ahead of us cannot be compared with what lies within us.

Success is first within and then without. Several inner factors determine our outward success. For example, courage is an inner force. Courage does not always roar. At times, it is just a quiet voice at the end of the day, saying, "I will try again tomorrow." It's been said that it's not the size of the dog in the fight, but the size of the 'fight' in the dog that determines the ultimate victory.

A man, in an attempt to teach his son courage, told the lad: "when life knocks you down, make sure you land on your back, because if you land on your back, you can look up, and if you can look up, you can get up. It is the spirit of courage that declares "it is not over until it's over, and it's not over until I win."

You were not designed for defeat. You were configured for dominion and destined for greatness. But to win in life, you have got to keep on keeping on. The race doesn't always go to the swift but to those who keep on moving. It is the hammer of persistence that ultimately drives in the nail of success.

Courage says "never say never," for those who say "it cannot be done" are usually interrupted by someone already doing it. Neither the length of the journey, nor the strength of the opposition can break the will of the truly courageous.

With a will, you can win. With guts, you can leave the rut. With a heart, you can make a mark. With determination, you will reach your destination. How do we develop courage? Simply put, by making up our minds. Nothing is as powerful as the power of a made-up mind.

Never settle for what is available at the expense of what is possible. When the going gets tough and rough, the tough gets going. What challenges are you currently facing? They are not enough to make you give up on your dreams. Make up your mind to survive. If you will dare to survive, you are sure to arrive. Get up and get going. There is greatness in your future. You will get there in Jesus' name.

## FIRST THINGS FIRST

Man was created with an instinct to worship, fellowship and dominate. You sure need God in your life. The greatest decision you can ever make is to accept the Lordship of Jesus into your life as this has an implication on your life here on earth and hereafter. Have you accepted Jesus into your life? Are you born again? If you are not sure, say these words:

"Lord Jesus, I believe you died on the cross, and was buried and rose again from death because of me. I come to you today. I am a sinner and cannot help myself. Forgive me my sins. Cleanse me with your blood. Today, I accept You as my Lord and Saviour. Thank you for saving me. Amen.

Dear friend, welcome to the family of God. Be free to be a part of God's people around you.

I will love to read from you.
E-mail: reveboda@gmail.com
Twitter: @niyieboda
Facebook: Gbeminiyi Eboda

# OTHER
# BOOKS

## BY

## THE
## AUTHOR

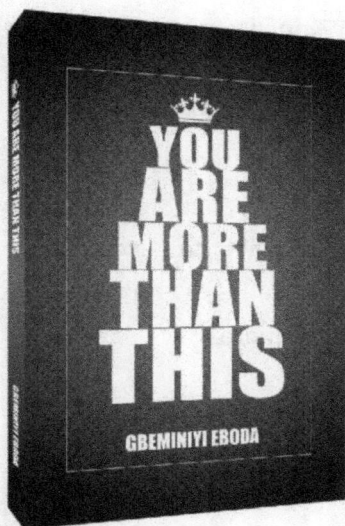

There's no barrier to success. It's all about you. This book will help you find a way out of ignorance and develop a very strong database that will usher you into the future that you have always dreamt of.

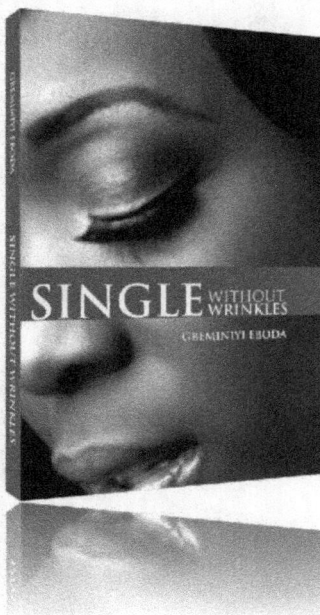

A toast to every spinster, the truth for every bachelor. This book is God's wisdom delicately packaged for the lady to disentangle her from the web of influences and past experiences hindering her from being maximised.

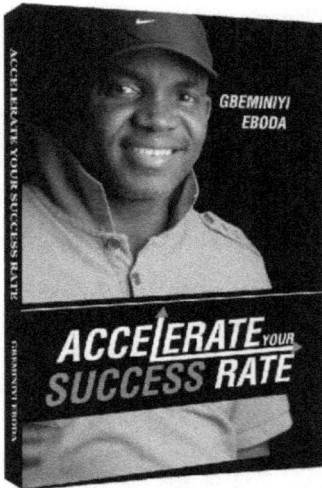

"The impossible is the untried". This book is suitable for individuals and organisations who will dare the odds and venture the impossible to become more and do more and ultimately have more.

This text is another archetypal to guide you from living a life of activity into a life of higher productivity!

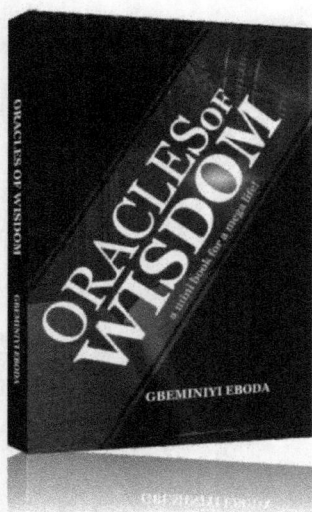

In this book are wisdom nuggets covering different aspects of life. It's a mini book for a mega life!

You are the main character in this book! This text is a blueprint or guide which if followed will take you from where you are to where you want and passionately desire to be in life and the whole concept is to help unearth the value on your inside from its potential form.

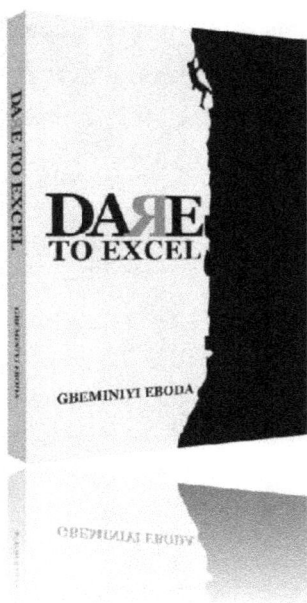

Success requires that you believe in God, yourself and the dream. These are wisdom tips packaged for a forward-focused dreamer on his way to achieving greatness.